Tornado

Catherine Chambers

Heinemann Library
Chicago, Illinois

Customer Service 888-454-2279

Visit our website at www.heinemannlibrary.com

Designed by Visual Image
Illustration by Paul Bale
Originated by Ambassador Litho
Printed and bound in South China

06 05 04 03 02
10 9 8 7 6 5 4 3 2 1

Library of Congress Cataloging-in-Publication Data
Chambers, Catherine, 1954-
   Tornado / Catherine Chambers.
      p. cm. -- (Wild weather)
Summary: Describes how tornadoes are formed, the conditions that exist in tornadoes, the harmful and beneficial effects of these storms, and their impact on humans, plants, and animals.
Includes bibliographical references and index.
   ISBN 1-58810-652-7 (HC), 1-4034-0116-0 (Pbk)
   1. Tornadoes--Juvenile literature. 2. Tornadoes--Physiological effect--Juvenile literature. [1. Tornadoes.] I. Title. II. Series.
   QC955.2 .C478 2002
   551.55'3--dc21
                            2002000823

Acknowledgments
The author and publishers are grateful to the following for permission to reproduce copyright material: pp. 8, 14, 19, 20, 23, 27, 28 Associated Press: pp. 21, 25 Corbis; p. 22 FLPA; pp. 4, 11, 15 Oxford Scientific Films; p. 26 PA Photos; p. 16 Photodisc; p. 12 Rex Features; p. 5 Robert Harding Picture Library; pp. 10, 13, 18 Science Photo Library; pp. 7, 9, 17, 24, 29 Stone.
Cover photograph reproduced with permission of Imagestate.
The Publishers would like to thank the Met Office for their assistance with the preparation of this book.
Every effort has been made to contact copyright holders of any material reproduced in this book. Any omissions will be rectified in subsequent printings if notice is given to the publisher.

Some words are shown in bold, **like this.** You can find out what they mean by looking in the glossary.

Contents

What Is a Tornado?

A tornado is a moving, spinning **funnel** of wind. It swirls down from dark, towering clouds. The wind in a tornado is very strong. The tornado can suck up anything in its path.

Everything sucked up by the tornado gets
thrown out at the sides as it moves along. This
makes a huge cloud of dust and **debris** around
the tornado.

Where Do Tornadoes Happen?

Tornadoes can happen anywhere, but they are more common in some places. This map shows the parts of the world where tornadoes are often seen. There are many tornadoes in the United States.

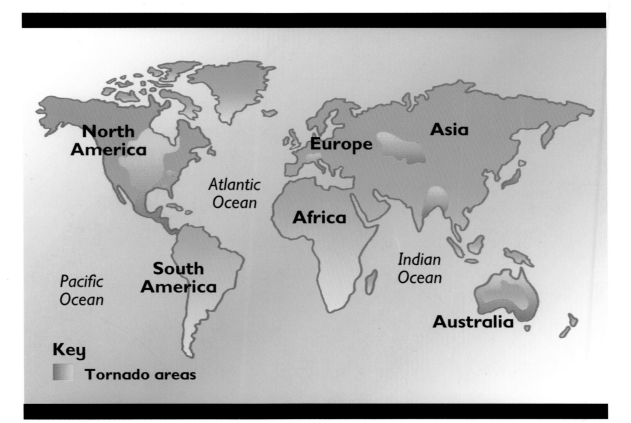

North America

Europe

Asia

Atlantic Ocean

Africa

South America

Indian Ocean

Pacific Ocean

Australia

Key

Tornado areas

Tornado Alley is the name given to a large
area in the middle of the United States. More
tornadoes happen here than anywhere else in
the world.

Wind and Clouds

Wind is caused by **masses** of air moving around. Some masses are cold. Others are warm. Warm air usually rises, and cold air rushes in to fill the space it leaves. This causes strong winds.

There is always **water vapor** in the air. When the air becomes cold enough, the vapor turns back into water and forms clouds. Tornadoes come from some of these clouds.

Why Do Tornadoes Happen?

Most tornadoes happen in hot, moist weather. Heavy storm clouds suck up warm, moist air from below. Cool air blows across the tops of the clouds. These movements make a twisting wind.

The spinning wind makes a cone-shaped **funnel**
that can reach all the way down to the ground.
When one of these funnels happens over water,
it is called a **waterspout.**

What Are Tornadoes Like?

People can see most tornadoes coming because of all the dust and **debris** swirling around the bottom of the **funnel.** But even if you can see a tornado, it is hard to tell exactly where it will go.

Sometimes a tornado happens as part of a thunderstorm. These storms have thunder, lightning, heavy rain, and strong winds.

Harmful Tornadoes

The winds in tornadoes travel faster than any other winds. They can destroy anything in their path, including buildings. They usually affect just a narrow area.

Some dark tornado clouds hold icy **hailstones.**
When the hailstones fall, they can hurt people
and animals. They can also damage buildings
and **crops.**

Tornado Alley

Oklahoma is in the middle of the United States. It is part of Tornado Alley. A lot of tornadoes happen here because the land is so flat. The wind sweeps across the **plains.**

A series of terrible tornadoes hit Oklahoma City on May 3, 1999. They destroyed everything in their paths. The flying **debris** hit people and buildings, and 45 people were killed.

Preparing for a Tornado

Weather **forecasters** keep a careful eye on the weather. When tornadoes are likely to happen, they send out a "tornado watch." If a tornado has been seen, they send out a "tornado warning."

Storm chasers are people who try to get close to tornadoes. The storm chasers take pictures of the tornadoes. Sometimes they are the first to send out a warning about a tornado.

Tornado Warning

On April 3, 1974, weather **forecasters** in the United States knew that the weather was perfect for tornadoes. They sent out more than 160 warnings to 14 states.

On that day, 148 tornadoes were reported in 13 states. More than 300 people were killed and at least 30,000 buildings were destroyed. No one could stop the tornadoes.

Coping with Tornadoes

Tornadoes can damage all types of buildings. In some places, people are able to go to special **shelters** when they know a tornado is coming. These shelters are often under the ground.

You should never stay in a car when a tornado strikes. Tornado winds are so powerful that they can pick up cars and throw them high into the air.

Tornadoes and Nature

There are many stories of frogs falling from the sky during storms. This is because they can get sucked up by tornadoes. They fall to the ground again when the tornado is over.

Tornadoes often blow across fields where **crops** are grown. They can destroy the crops that lie in their path. The paths of some tornadoes are wider than the length of a football field.

To the Rescue!

After a tornado, rescuers often find people trapped in their cars or underneath flattened buildings. Ambulances rush **injured** people to the hospital.

Emergency tornado **shelters** can protect people from tornadoes. They are stronger than most houses and other buildings. A tornado's winds cannot destroy these shelters.

Adapting to Tornadoes

People who live where tornadoes often happen must learn how to take **shelter.** Here, some children are having a **tornado drill** at school.

It is important to know what to do if a tornado
strikes. In most houses the basement is the
safest place to hide. At school your teachers
will tell you where to go.

Fact File

◆ At least 1,000 tornadoes hit the United States each year. More than half of them happen in the spring, and about a quarter in the summer. More tornadoes happen in April than any other month.

◆ Most tornadoes happen in the afternoon. This is because afternoons are usually the warmest part of the day. The heat helps clouds to form.

◆ Scientists use invisible **radio signals** to find out if a tornado is forming. The signals bounce off **ice crystals** in the clouds. Then the signals make a pattern on a computer screen. If the pattern makes a hook shape, a tornado is probably forming.

Glossary

crop plant that is grown for food

debris earth and broken objects that are thrown around by a tornado

forecaster someone who collects information about the weather in order to predict what kind of weather we will get

funnel long, thin, cone-shaped tube

hailstone small ball of ice that comes from some thunderclouds

ice crystal tiny piece of frozen water

injure to hurt someone

mass large amount of something like air that does not have a definite shape

plain large area of flat land

radio signal wave of sound that travels through the air

shelter place where people can go to be safe

tornado drill practice in what to do during a tornado

waterspout huge spout of water made when a funnel cloud forms over a body of water

water vapor water that has changed into a gas

31

More Books to Read

Ashwell, Miranda, and Andy Owen. *Wind*. Chicago: Heinemann Library, 1999.

Hayden, Kate. *Twisters!* New York: Dorling Kindersley Publishing, Inc., 2000.

Simon, Seymour. *Tornadoes*. New York: HarperCollins Children's Book Group, 2001.

Index